WHOLE WIDE WORLD
EIFFEL TOWER

by Kristine Spanier, MLIS

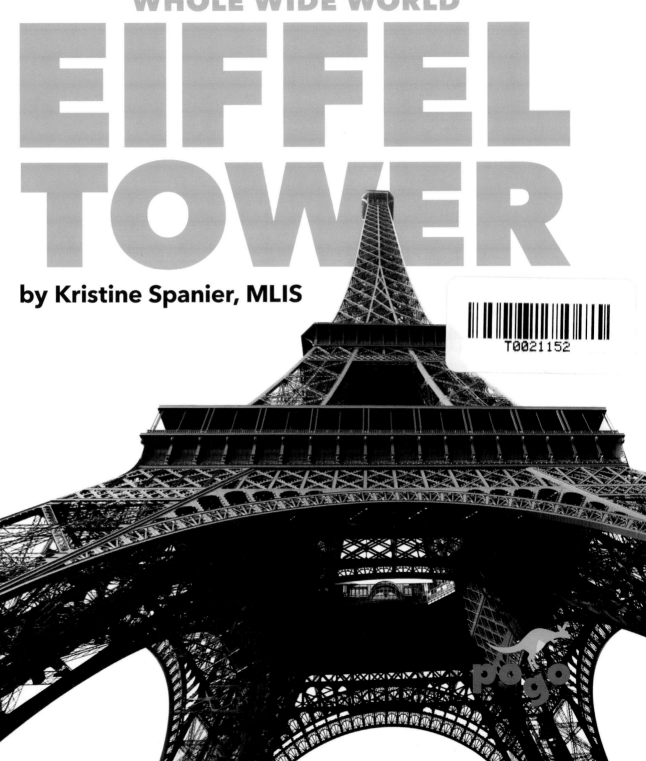

pogo

Ideas for Parents and Teachers

Pogo Books let children practice reading informational text while introducing them to nonfiction features such as headings, labels, sidebars, maps, and diagrams, as well as a table of contents, glossary, and index.

Carefully leveled text with a strong photo match offers early fluent readers the support they need to succeed.

Before Reading

- "Walk" through the book and point out the various nonfiction features. Ask the student what purpose each feature serves.
- Look at the glossary together. Read and discuss the words.

Read the Book

- Have the child read the book independently.
- Invite him or her to list questions that arise from reading.

After Reading

- Discuss the child's questions. Talk about how he or she might find answers to those questions.
- Prompt the child to think more. Ask: People worldwide recognize the Eiffel Tower as a symbol of France. Is there an important symbol where you live?

Pogo Books are published by Jump!
5357 Penn Avenue South
Minneapolis, MN 55419
www.jumplibrary.com

Library of Congress Cataloging-in-Publication Data

Names: Spanier, Kristine, author.
Title: Eiffel tower / Kristine Spanier.
Description: Minneapolis: Jump!, Inc., [2021]
Series: Whole wide world
Includes index. | Audience: Ages 7-10
Identifiers: LCCN 2020025800 (print)
LCCN 2020025801 (ebook)
ISBN 9781645277354 (hardcover)
ISBN 9781645277361 (paperback)
ISBN 9781645277378 (ebook)
Subjects: LCSH: Tour Eiffel (Paris, France)—Juvenile literature. Building, Iron and steel—Juvenile literature.
Classification: LCC NA2930 .S694 2021 (print)
LCC NA2930 (ebook) | DDC 725/.970944361—dc23
LC record available at https://lccn.loc.gov/2020025800
LC ebook record available at https://lccn.loc.gov/2020025801

Editor: Jenna Gleisner
Designer: Molly Ballanger

Photo Credits: Matthew Dixon/Shutterstock, cover; Roman Sigaev/Shutterstock, 1; Sergey Novikov/Shutterstock, 3; bancika/Shutterstock, 4; engel. ac/Shutterstock, 5; Hulton Archive/Getty, 6-7; S-F/Shutterstock, 8-9; pisaphotography/Shutterstock, 10; Three Lions/Getty, 11; FL Collection 2/Alamy, 12-13; Science History Images/Alamy, 14-15; Dennis van de Water/Shutterstock, 16; Ingus Kruklitis/Dreamstime, 17; Hanohiki/Dreamstime, 18-19tl; Byron Ortiz/Shutterstock, 18-19tr; WhiteLife/Shutterstock, 18-19bl; Blue Planet Studio/Shutterstock, 18-19br; Pawel Libera/Getty, 20-21; ALEX_UGALEK/Shutterstock, 23.

Printed in the United States of America at Corporate Graphics in North Mankato, Minnesota.

TABLE OF CONTENTS

. . . .

CHAPTER 1

PARIS'S TOWER

Take elevators more than 900 feet (274 meters) high. Step outside. See as far as 40 miles (64 kilometers). You are at the top of the Eiffel Tower! It is in Paris, France.

Paris, France

platform

This tower was built in just over two years! It stands on four legs. It is made of **latticed** steel. There are three viewing platforms.

platform

platform

Paris is France's **capital**. It hosted the 1889 world's fair. A contest was held to design a **monument** for it. Gustave Eiffel was an **engineer**. His team won.

DID YOU KNOW?

Eiffel was called the "magician of iron." He created hundreds of metal **structures**. Many were railroad bridges. He also designed the **framework** of the Statue of Liberty!

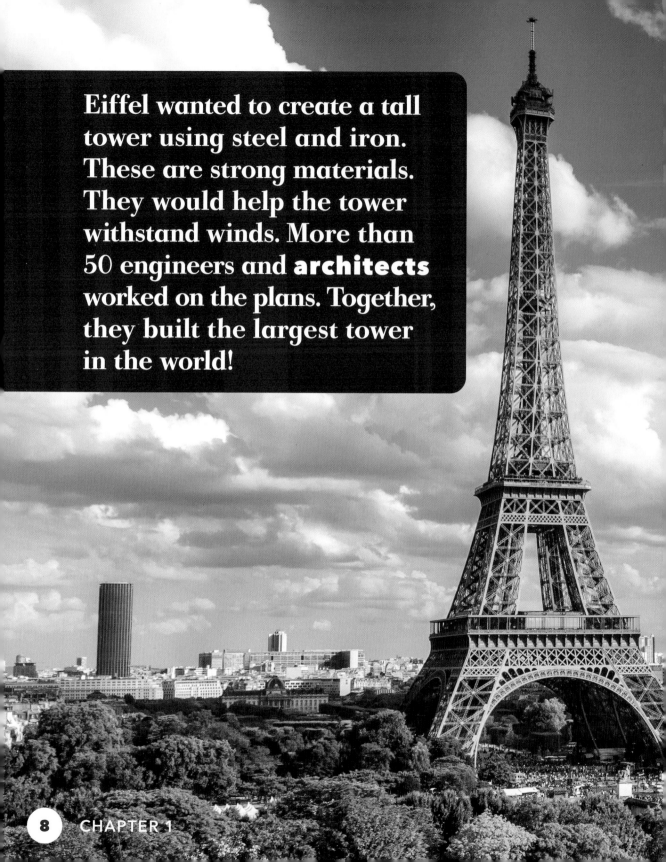

Eiffel wanted to create a tall tower using steel and iron. These are strong materials. They would help the tower withstand winds. More than 50 engineers and **architects** worked on the plans. Together, they built the largest tower in the world!

TAKE A LOOK!

The Eiffel Tower is no longer the tallest tower in the world. See how it compares!

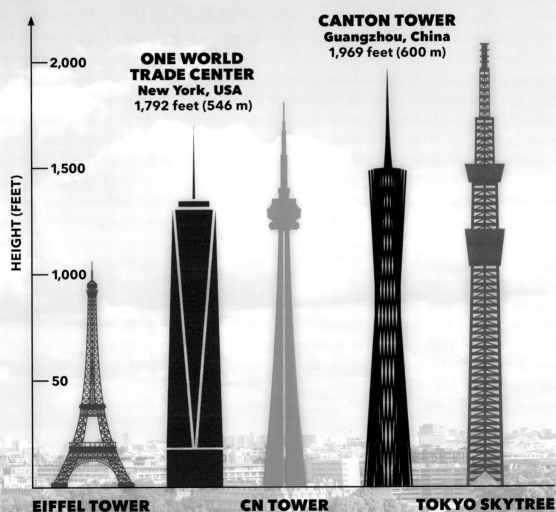

ONE WORLD TRADE CENTER
New York, USA
1,792 feet (546 m)

CANTON TOWER
Guangzhou, China
1,969 feet (600 m)

HEIGHT (FEET)

2,000

1,500

1,000

50

EIFFEL TOWER
Paris, France
1,063 feet (324 m)

CN TOWER
Toronto, Canada
1,815 feet (553 m)

TOKYO SKYTREE
Tokyo, Japan
2,080 feet (634 m)

CHAPTER 2

BUILDING THE TOWER

There are 18,000 pieces to the tower. They are held together with **rivets**. There are 2.5 million of them on the tower! It took four people to install each one.

rivet

Sections of the tower were built at a factory. At least 150 workers helped.

August 1887

October 1887

April 1888

July 1888

November 1888

March 1889

It took five months to build the **foundations**. It took 21 months to finish the tower. This was record time!

The tower opened at the 1889 world's fair. It took 10 more days for the elevators to work. People didn't want to wait. More than 30,000 people walked to the top. They had to climb 1,710 steps!

WHAT DO YOU THINK?

A world's fair shows off **inventions** from around the world. Visitors enjoy arts, crafts, and food, too. What if you could invent something for a world's fair? What would it be?

CHAPTER 3

THE TOWER TODAY

antenna ·····▶

The tower was supposed to stand for just 20 years. But Eiffel had an **antenna** put on top. It **transmitted** the first French public radio program in 1925. This made the tower useful. It now has 120 antennas!

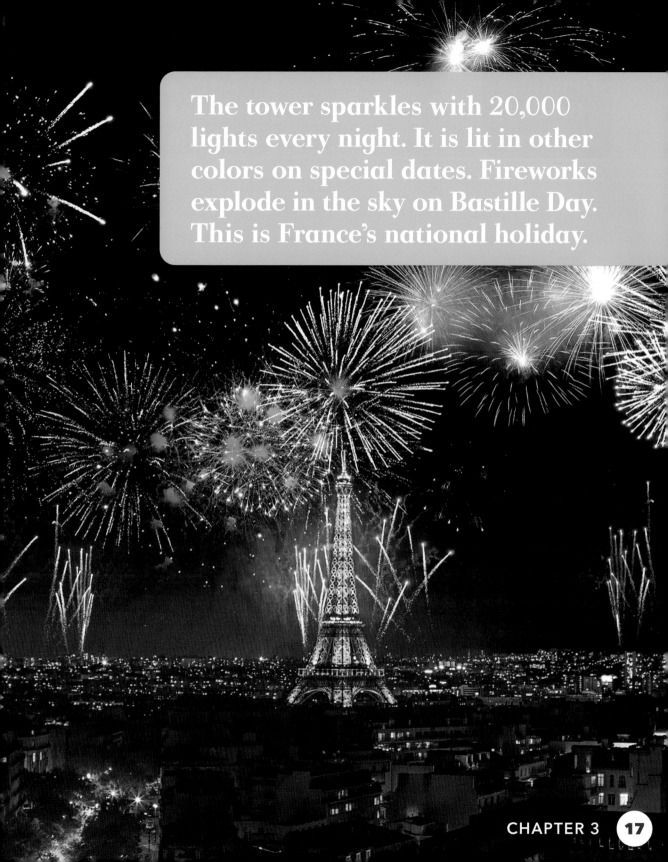

The tower sparkles with 20,000 lights every night. It is lit in other colors on special dates. Fireworks explode in the sky on Bastille Day. This is France's national holiday.

Funkturm Berlin, Germany

Torre del Reformador, Guatemala

Eiffel Tower replica, Pakistan

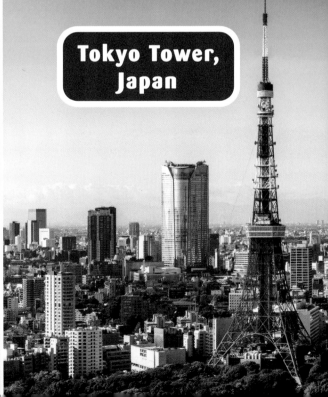

Tokyo Tower, Japan

The tower has been copied more than 50 times. The copies are all around the world. Some are taller. Some are shorter. Some are a different color. But they stand out in the **skyline** just like the original!

WHAT DO YOU THINK?

What if you could build a tower? Would you copy a popular idea? Or would you come up with a new one? Why?

The Eiffel Tower is a **symbol** of France. It is in paintings and movies. It has inspired writers and musicians. Millions of people visit it every year! Would you like to visit it?

QUICK FACTS & TOOLS

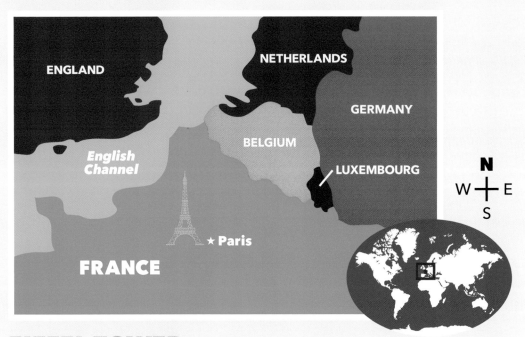

ENGLAND

NETHERLANDS

GERMANY

BELGIUM

LUXEMBOURG

English Channel

★ Paris

FRANCE

N
W E
S

EIFFEL TOWER

Location: Paris, France

Height: 1,063 feet (324 m)

Years Built: 1887 to 1889

Primary Architect:
Stephen Sauvestre

Primary Engineers:
Gustave Eiffel, Maurice Koechlin,
and Emile Nouguier

Past Use: gateway to world's
fair, radio transmitter, science
laboratory

Current Use: tourist attraction,
media transmitter

**Number of Visitors
Each Year:** around 7 million

GLOSSARY

antenna: A device that receives radio and television signals.

architects: People who design buildings and supervise the way they are built.

capital: The city in a country or state where the government is based.

engineer: Someone who is specially trained to design and build machines or large structures.

foundations: Solid structures on which buildings or towers are constructed.

framework: A structure that gives shape or support to something.

inventions: Products or processes that are made after studies and experiments.

latticed: Having a framework or structure of crossed wood or metal strips.

monument: A statue, building, or other structure that reminds people of an event or a person.

rivets: Short metal pins or bolts that are used to fasten pieces of metal together.

skyline: The outline of buildings, mountains, or other objects seen against the sky from a distance.

structures: Things that have been built.

symbol: An object that stands for, suggests, or represents something else.

transmitted: Sent out radio or television signals.

INDEX

TO LEARN MORE

Finding more information is as easy as 1, 2, 3.

1. **Go to www.factsurfer.com**
2. **Enter "EiffelTower" into the search box.**
3. **Choose your book to see a list of websites.**

FACT SURFER